Unspoken Words

Unspoken Words

An Open Diary

FAREEDA A. WASHINGTON

UNSPOKEN WORDS
AN OPEN DIARY

iUniverse books may be ordered through booksellers or by contacting:

iUniverse
1663 Liberty Drive
Bloomington, IN 47403
www.iuniverse.com
844-349-9409

Because of the dynamic nature of the Internet, any web addresses or links contained in this book may have changed since publication and may no longer be valid. The views expressed in this work are solely those of the author and do not necessarily reflect the views of the publisher, and the publisher hereby disclaims any responsibility for them.

Any people depicted in stock imagery provided by Getty Images are models, and such images are being used for illustrative purposes only. Certain stock imagery © Getty Images.

ISBN: 978-1-6632-3314-1 (sc)
ISBN: 978-1-6632-3315-8 (e)

Library of Congress Control Number: 2021924915

Print information available on the last page.

iUniverse rev. date: 12/14/2021

This collection of memories, thoughts, and experiences is dedicated to the little girl inside every woman who could not find her voice to speak of her pain, to everyone who helped me find my voice along the way, and to the memory of my bother Jamal A. Washington Sr., my inspiration.

Contents

Part 3: Love

Part 4: Evolution

Part 5: Self

Introduction

A letter from The Author

Poetry saved my life. When I was 14 years old, I wrote my first poem. I picked up a piece of paper and a pencil and wrote out my thoughts and feelings. I am not sure if something I had read or heard inspired me, but I managed to put words together that made sense. I wrote the poem probably in less than half an hour. Pleased with myself, I gave it to my mother to read. I walked away and went into my room to wait for her reaction. I was nervous, excited, and eager to hear what she thought about it. I was sure that she would be as impressed and as proud as I was.

I do not know if she read the entire poem. It was not very long, but after what seemed like only a minute, she came busting into my room. I had seen that look on her face before; she was upset! The scowl across her face was not at all what I was expecting. All that I remember was being so confused and surprised that I could barely make out the words that she said. What I could piece together was that she was doing her best and how dare I complain that "times are hard"! She said more words before leaving the room just as quickly as she had entered. I re-read the poem repeatedly that night, trying to come to some understanding of her perspective of what she had read. To me, my words were about hope and survival. I thought the poem was encouraging. To her, maybe my speaking of hard times and our struggles felt more like criticism. I am not sure, but one thing that I was sure of was that my words provoked that emotion from her. At 14, I did not understand how much power was in my words.

Words have the power to evoke emotions from those who hear and read them. What I came to know is that my truth is MY truth, and everyone experiences things differently. Shared experiences can have a different impact on each person. It is not my place to deny, challenge, or question someone else's truth. It is more important that I am aware of, acknowledge, and stand on my own thoughts, feelings, morals, and beliefs.

As a young girl, I was oblivious that my ability to create poetry was a gift. This gift helped me through life. I sometimes lose the confidence to express myself verbally. Not expressing myself became a habit. That habit forced me to hold things inside. Writing provided me an outlet to convey disappointment, loss, love, loss of love, and everything that I have experienced thus far. It helps me process my journey as I am discovering who I am becoming. Writing saves me from suffocating inside.

My mother knew that life wasn't always pleasant for little girls, so she was overly protective of me. I remember her saying that she would protect me at all costs, and I knew she was telling the truth. If my friends had fathers or brothers in the home, I could not hang out at their houses. Spending the night anywhere other than my grandmother's house was out of the question. Because of my mother's protection, I spent much of my young life feeling alone, even though I was surrounded by family. Being alone wasn't a bad thing. I became comfortable being by myself and sometimes preferred it.

I am the only girl of five children. I have four brothers, two older and two younger. This, in and of itself, made me the oddball. A middle child. The age difference between me and my brothers was enough that I had to go through school alone. I was too young to hang out with my older brothers, and I was too old to hang out with my younger brothers. Plus, I was a girl! Even though we all enjoyed sports and video games, somehow those common interests were never enough to bring us together. We love each other dearly, but at that age we did not want to hang out with each other. Without the freedom to hang out with my friends, I was often isolated.

Before I explored writing, I developed a love for playing basketball. Basketball allotted me the opportunity to meet people, socialize, and build friendships. I wanted to play all the time, but after a certain age, my girlfriends were not trying to spend every day of the summer outside playing basketball. Boys in the neighborhood played every day, so I would play with them. That did not last long. Mama said they were not really playing defense but were trying to touch on me, so she ran them off. I was alone again! As a teenager, I missed out on house parties, going to the movies at Cinemark, hanging out at Indian Springs Mall, going to Skateland, swimming at Parkwood Pool, and most other things that kids my age were doing. I know my mother was protecting me the best way that she knew how. I do not blame her for that. When I became a mother, I understood more. I know that as much fun as I feel I missed out on, I may have also escaped things that may not have been good for me. Even so, it still created a very lonely feeling in my childhood.

To escape this loneliness, I picked up another hobby outside of basketball. I read. Since I had very little social life, I found it intriguing to read about other people's lives. Hours would pass by as I escaped my reality and became lost in an alternative one. I spent most of my days in the summer going to the library and checking out 3-4 books at once. When I finished with them, I would go back and get more. I estimate I probably read close to 20-30 books and magazines every summer. While reading different authors like Maya Angelou, Terry McMillan, Eric Jerome Dickey, Omar Tyree, and so many others, I fell in love with words and the way writers would put words together to create stories.

I have always been an observer, a listener, and a thinker. As a child, I was quiet. Being quiet allowed me to offer a safe place for people to speak at. I say speak at because as a child I rarely shared my advice, opinions, or thoughts. Maybe because I was afraid that I would hurt someone's feelings or be seen as disrespectful if I did not agree with them. I did not feel that there was space for a child's opinion. So instead, I listened. I would listen to what they did not say, and I would put together the pieces. I wrote about the things that others poured into me. I observed life, then I wrote. I internalized life, then I wrote. I experienced life, then I wrote. I am grateful that they trusted me to be a gatekeeper to their secrets. It conditioned me to know life through different points of view and when I found my voice, I could offer solutions based on knowledge. Getting these thoughts and emotions out saved my life in the sense that it allowed me to not suffocate on the words that I did not have the courage to speak.

I am just learning how to speak of things that I have held inside of my heart for so long. Before I found my voice, I wrote. These are those unspoken words. This is a collection of thoughts and feelings that I have never shared before. This is my truth. It is not always easy to share or receive the truth, but I hope my truth offers a different perspective on shared experiences for those who have been on this journey with me. My purpose is to help heal, encourage, support, and love those who need it. Each experience has helped to mold me and condition me for my work of service to others. These experiences are from different points of my journey, life lessons that became blessings. I pray these words live within you and bring forth feelings of empowerment and wholeness. May my words provide a sense of belonging, understanding, and love to anyone that has experienced life in a similar way.

With Love,
Free

PART I

Life

Life: Living Ain't Easy

Life can be hard; it can be beautiful, and it can be ugly. Life can bring about amazing highs and shattering lows. It comprises happiness and delivers pain. My spiritual father often says, "if you have not been through anything, keep living." Life happens and you cannot stop it. Most of us just absorb it. How can you be good when things in life are bad? How does one hold on to a smile and pure heart when life seems to be against you? I am taught to treat my valleys and my peaks the same because they are both just temporary. The one thing that I hold on to always is hope.

For as far back as I can remember, my mother talked to us about life. About the traps that were waiting for us if we did not pay attention. As a child, my mother was the biggest influence in my life. What I recognized is that my mother is a survivor. She could write a book about the many obstacles that she had to overcome. I am grateful to have a mother that was open enough to share her story for the sake of saving me from self-destruction. I did not have to make certain mistakes because she revealed to me the struggles that came with those choices. She taught me and my brothers the game and how to survive it. She talked to us about dating, hustling, drugs, sex, respect, the importance of finishing school, and any and everything else. There was no topic that was off limits. My mother has always possessed wisdom, street smarts, and common sense. She has always demanded respect and receives it. I learned a lot from her about how to move through the world. She has a gift, an ability to relate to people. Her realness and openness draw people to her. I believe she and I share that gift.

Watching my mother taught me how to survive. She taught me that showing respect for myself and others would take me far in life. She does not believe in disrespecting elders. My mother, being raised in the home with her grandparents, was taught "yes ma'am", "no ma'am", "yes sir", and "no sir", before she got out in the streets at 16 years old. She passed those same morals down to her children. She lived a fast life, and she did not want that for me, her only daughter. I always felt that it was important to live the life my mother wanted me to live. The life that she wanted for herself. She wanted me to be a good girl. I am who I am today, largely because of her. As parents with limited resources, she and my father did the best that they could for us. Nevertheless, there was always a desire inside of me to want more. To want something different from what I knew. I did not always know how to be better, but along the way, people came into my life to show me how.

When I look back over my life, I cannot help but be humbled and grateful about where I am today. I was born and raised in Belrose Manor section 8 housing projects, before moving to 11th & Rowland in the early 1990s. I lived one block from the infamous Quindaro Boulevard, located in the heart of inner-city Kansas City, KS. During that time, the community was full of violence, drugs, drug addicts, prostitutes, and poverty. I also saw people who were entrepreneurs, and those that got up and went to work every day. Growing up in that environment taught me I had to work hard if I wanted a different life for myself. Life would only be as good as I made it with the help of God.

I remember having a conversation with a friend about my perspective growing up. We grew up in the same neighborhood but had unique experiences. I told him how sometimes we went without lights or gas. Sometimes, we didn't have enough food to eat. I shared having a gun pulled out on me and my brother when I was around 12 years old because the guy didn't like how my brother was looking at him. We talked about how I got into fights almost every summer. His response was that my experience was "normal". That statement did not sit well with me. These things should not be normal, although unfortunately, it may be typical in that environment. My insides cried out, "No, that isn't normal!" I will no longer allow it to be. I became determined to create a new normal for my child. I knew the bad sides of things all too well. Those instances molded my outlook on life and how I view the world today.

Imagine me, 15 years old, picking out my clothes at night, preparing for school the next day. Before I went to bed, I laid there listening to the "Quiet Storm" on the radio. It is mostly quiet in the house other than the voices of my parents and their friends who were downstairs visiting in the living room. My younger siblings had already gone to bed. Eventually, I drifted off to a peaceful sleep. Not long after, a consistently loud ringing noise in my ear abruptly awakened me.

I was frightened and startled. The noise did not cease. I was disoriented. What was happening!? My body froze for half of a second and I jumped up out of bed and hid in the closet. My instinct told me that I was in danger. My mind was cloudy, and I could comprehend nothing. I could not hear over the loud ringing noise. I was not sure if I was breathing. I never experienced anything like this. I thought that the world was ending. Finally, after what seemed like forever, the noise stopped, and I gained some sense of awareness. I ran out of the dark closet and down the stairs to find my parents because I feared that they did not have time to seek shelter.

My heart was racing, my mouth was dry as cotton, my palms were sweating. When I reached the platform at the top of the stairs, I did not know what to expect, so I braced myself. A thousand questions were running through my mind. Are my parents still alive? Will I find their bodies covered in blood laying on the floor? Did only one of them survive, or did my brothers and I just become orphans? All these thoughts and fears ran through me in a millisecond. I still could not hear. I think I was in shock.

I saw my mother rushing to the door. I was alarmed because I was not sure if we were out of danger. My fear heightened; my entire body tensed. What if she was running into more danger? My father must have thought the same thing because he was trying to pull her away from the door. Why was she being so irrational, so careless? I wanted to yell at her to stop, but nothing would come out. I could not get my mouth to form a sound. What was waiting for us on the other side of that door? When the door opened, my older brother rushed into the house. My mom had opened the door despite the danger, to rescue her child. She was not thinking. There was no time to reason. She was acting the way any mother would who knew their child was in danger. Over the gunfire, she heard him call out to her. When my mother saw him, she dropped to her knees and vomited. This was her body's response to what we just experienced. My mind slowly made sense of this. I saw my brother, my mother, my father, and their friends. Everyone was okay, nobody was hurt. My legs gave out from under me. I fell on my butt at the top of the stairs and my body convulsed. I still could not hear; I remember the silence.

Later that night, we assessed the damage. There were so many bullet holes that had torn through our home. The damage was immeasurable. I went to my brother, we hugged but neither of us cried. He showed me a bullet hole. There was a hole through the vest that he was wearing near the stomach area. The bullet went through his hoodie, through the t-shirt and left a hole in his tank top, but there was not a scratch on his skin. We shook our heads in disbelief.

The next morning, there was a moving truck backed up to the front door. Anything that we owned that was not damaged by the hundreds of bullets that ruptured our foundation, we threw in the back of the truck. We did not pack; we just threw our things in the truck and left that day. As a result, we were homeless, living with family and friends, sleeping on floors and in hotels for six months. Some of our clothes were in the trunk of our car and we kept everything else we owned in storage.

I realized how dangerous people in the world could be, having no regard for life. I wanted revenge to come upon the people who brought harm to my family. For a long time, I walked around angry, not wanting to let that anger go. I kept telling myself, "Vengeance is mine, saith the Lord." I was not a churchgoer, so I am not sure where I heard that scripture, maybe in a movie, but I hoped it was true.

How do you move on from something like this? That experience made me not trust people. I do not remember telling any of my friends at the time about what happened. I am not sure if I was embarrassed or if it was because we did not discuss family business outside the home. I just remember that I did not talk about it much, with anyone. I became more alert, and even more humble. I retreated into my shell once again, a quiet little girl.

In response to feeling out of control, I became super focused. Despite my parents and I living in various locations. I remember still getting to school every day. Catching rides with different people, whoever I could. I even took a taxi at one point. I showed up every day for basketball practice. I had my best basketball season and got my best grades in school that year. I did not have control over the things that were happening around me, but I had control over my response. I did not allow what was happening to be an excuse for me not to show up and do my best. Instead, I put my energy into my studies, basketball, and writing. I knew school would be a ticket to a better future. Basketball was my joy; writing was my outlet. A safe place to express what was going on inside. This was my life, and I couldn't escape it. I made a choice to not allow this situation to throw me off track. I knew becoming bitter would be easy, but being better was my goal, so I stayed focused, not really knowing where I was going in life or how I was going to get there.

One thing about life is that it doesn't wait for anyone. Life doesn't stop and wait until you get it together. It continues to happen. I suffered the loss of loved ones. I loved romantically and was heartbroken. I tried my best to figure out my path with many failures. It can be very difficult to figure out who you are while the world tells you who they want you to be. I was 18 when life dealt me my next life shattering blow. Many years later, I would lose my dear friend Michelle to death by suicide and witness murder for the second time in my young life because of more gun violence. These things would come to affect my spirit and mental health. I was a walking time bomb and didn't know it. It's no surprise that all these things would lead me to a state of depression which I would deny for years.

Even with those challenges, life offered me many lessons of awareness, appreciation, compassion, and gratefulness. When things in life happen, it is important to have a support system in family and friends. People who will help you through. People who will encourage you. I could not find the words to speak about any of these things when they occurred, so I wrote. By the time I became an adult, the hurts, resentment, and anger were piled on top of each other. It felt like if I spoke about things, I would fall apart. The only way I felt safe was to write about them. I was not aware that all this built-up trauma was still living inside me, lying dormant because I had not permitted myself to address the woes of life. Everyone tells you to be strong. I didn't know it was okay to not be strong all the time.

My parents were trying to figure out how we could survive. I did not want to put my issues on them. I looked at it like giving someone a burden who was already carrying the weight of the world on their shoulders. I could have spoken to my friends, but to be honest, I did not think they would understand because none of them had gone through anything like this. I apologize for not allowing them to try. I may have caused myself to be alone in my grief, but when you are grieving and learning life at the same time, it is hard to see things outside of yourself. When you shut down, you are shutting people out and potentially blocking blessings such as help, support, healing words, or a listening ear. When you are blinded by the grief and the pain of life, sometimes you cannot even see God. God will always send help, but you must be open to receive it. When help comes, it may not be on your time or look like what you expect.

I think the worst experiences in my life have made me a stronger person. My maternal great grandmother, whom we lovingly called "Granny" would tell me "It could always be worse". Knowing that made me tell myself that whatever situation I was going through, there was someone, somewhere, that was going through something worse than me. I would immediately be grateful for what I had and what things were going right. I always had faith that things would be better. I did not have a terrible life; I just did not always have the best experiences.

Life is the greatest gift we possess. Even still, I know that my life is not my own and that I am here to serve others. I work hard in hopes of leaving an imprint in this world, that I do not live my life in vain. Some people will reach many, however, I believe many people are here to reach just one. That one life may be the one that touches many, but we all have a purpose. Whatever role you play, be the best at it, rather it is as a parent, sibling, child, teacher, coach, spouse, friend, employee, boss, etc. Let everything that you do in this life be with the purpose of becoming better and making those around you better, regardless of what obstacles are in your way.

I survived the pitfalls that were before me and made it to college. I played collegiate basketball on a scholarship and ultimately earned my degree. Later, I used my background and education to work within the juvenile justice system with youth from my community. I found that to be gratifying. I sit in meetings where I am the only person who looks like me and I know I am there for a reason. My life has uniquely equipped me to give a needed perspective that can affect change. I strive to introduce a different narrative of the people in the community that I am from. I try to reach as many youths as I can by letting them know that someone believes in them. I let them know that even though options may seem few, they can do whatever they choose to do. I believe that every human being has the potential to be great if they choose to tap into the greatness that is already inside. As I do my work, I am aware my purpose, place, and position are all by design. I don't take my life for granted.

Untitled
(THE FIRST POEM I EVER WROTE)

Just fourteen years old and I think I've been scarred
Because good times are little, and most times are hard.

As I know, everything could be worse,
Though I'm not superstitious
But it feels like a curse.

As I pray to the lord as he lays me down to sleep
And I crawl into bed underneath my sheets,

I asked God to bless me and make things alright,
To make me strong so I can stand on
my feet and put up a fight.

For no man and no situation to hold me down,
And If I should fall, shall I get up off the ground.

I may not have everything I want in the world,
But in my eyes that makes me a better girl.

For everything is not handed to me on a silver platter,
And that makes me work even harder
to get to the top of the ladder.

So now I see what I have in mind,
Because my "one woman's strength" is one of a kind.

And my parents I know that they do their best,
They go all year round without any rest.

Even though they may struggle to pay the rent,
But from God and my parents is where I get my strength.

And when I get older whenever I can,
I'll make a promise to myself
That I'll lend them a hand.

Pandemic

Mothers dying of the disease of grief
The smile on her face isn't a cure
It's just a Band-Aid to cover the ache inside

Tears either stirring up or easing pain
Sons snatched away,
Here today, gone today

Here in my heart forever
Yet no longer physically here,
I see you when I close my eyes
Hear your voice in my ear

Heart torn into a million pieces that will never
Be repaired
In this lifetime.

Love and Basketball

Couldn't call anybody who would consume
How I feel so I just started to write

Like Thanksgiving Day, Full
Like Christmas Day, Excitement
Like Valentine's Day, Love
Like Fourth of July, Fireworks

Was what it was like in the beginning. Now...

Like air, Without content
Like clear, No color
Like broken guitar strings, No music
Like darkness, No sight
Like silence, No sound
Like lost, No you

Is what it's like now.

A Depressed State of Mind

I've shaken hands with death, stared it in the face
Let it kiss me on the cheek and whisper in my ear,
I'm here
Always when I've least expected

Steals the air that I breathe
Never offering reasoning,
Leaving me
In a world that makes no sense
It
Knocked me down on my knees
Until I surrendered and showed it respect

Ain't no getting away from it
You got to stand in it
Ten toes down, chin up
And take the blow to the gut
It's gon' knock you down
But you better get back up
And allow sense back in your head

Dread being a living dead
Soul hurt
Soul search
Let go of tears
May take 5, 10, 20 years
But fight,
Fight!
To get back to life
And live again

Instead of
Existing in this state of restlessness,
Mind going in and out of dark places
Seeing strangers in familiar faces
Paranoid in safe places
Many times, I wanted to quit
Feeling this pain in my chest
If I don't allow HIM to take over
My soul will know
No rest

Death,
Itself, made me want to be more familiar with it
Made me call him uncle and beg him to take the hurt away
Fell out with God
Cried,
Screamed and kicked
Asked him why so many times have I had to go through this?
It's hard to find hope in hopelessness
It's hard to be whole in brokenness
But I just keep up the fight

For sanity,
For my life,
Does HE even remember me?
As I stretch to try to get this
Current existence to flee from my bones
Stretch and moan
Don't forsake me, please
God, don't leave me alone

During my agony,
I heard HIM speak to me,
He said my child, I'm here, I hear.
I know living ain't easy but believe in me
I will never leave you nor forsake you
I have pitied your every groan,
You are my child,
Now lay every burden down
For where you are weak,
I am strong.

Keeping Count

1 life crushed by
2 years of pain
3 months carried your child
4 times we broke up because things had changed
5 months we were fine
6 years you were with her while
7 times we traveled to see each other
8 hours divided us
9 months and she had your baby
10 times more, I loved you
11 brothers, uncles and cousins wanted to kick your ass
12 months equal 1 year gone past

PART II

Heartbreak

Heartbreak: Suffering in Silence

I remember my cousin sharing that her aunt told her "Everyone has a story." That stuck with me at the time. Hearing this reminded me that pain is not unique. The stories of my pain are shared by many and for some, their stories are worse. I told myself, I do not get to use my pain or experiences as reasons not to do my best in this life. At the time, I did not know that I also needed to give myself permission to process my pain. I did not learn that lesson until years later.

I've both witnessed and experienced heartbreak. As early as the age of seven, I remember a young neighborhood teen being gunned downed in front of our apartment. I remember his mother, crouched over his body, crying tears that only a mother who has lost a child so tragically could relate to. I remember his brother, crying, broken, distraught from losing probably his best friend. As I watched them from the window, I remember feeling sorry that they were going through that heartbreak.

When I was a little older, I watched my mother lose her father to cancer. She adored her father, as much as I do mine. She was a daddy's girl, and her father was the closest person she had lost up to that point. Watching my mother,

I remember feeling sympathy for her broken heart. At 12 years old I did not understand loss. I was sad because my mother was sad. I knew my grandfather, but we did not have a close relationship. It was not until years later that I would experience the type of pain that would break my heart. Six years later to be exact.

Not all heartbreak results from romantic relationships. I believe that heartbreak is only possible as it relates to the loss of great love. Heartbreak can be the result of losing a game you love, losing a friend you love, a family member, or even a pet. Love and heartbreak go hand-in-hand. Yet the pain feels different depending on the relationship.

Nothing could have prepared me for January 5th, 2002. I was away from home for my first year of college. I had gotten a scholarship to play basketball at a community college that was three hours away. I was on my own for the first time trying to figure out life. The college was in a small town and there was not a lot of trouble to get into. I was not homesick because by this time I preferred to be by myself. I was close enough to home to go back with friends on some weekends and holiday breaks to visit my family. I think my mother took me being away from home harder than I did. Often when I would talk to her, she would say, "you don't have to stay there, you can come home." To me, coming home was not an option. I knew that this was my only chance to further my education which could open doors to new opportunities. I also loved that I got a chance to continue to play basketball, which by this time I'd fallen in love with.

During winter break I went home to spend time with my family. I remember my brother Jamal and I had a great time. He was five years older than me, but I think he was starting to see me as more than just his baby sister. He was living with his girlfriend and young baby boy. He was working and had bought me an outfit for Christmas. This was the first gift he ever bought me. For New Year's it had become a tradition for the family to bring in the new year together. My brother and I had a great time again, enjoying each other's company as adults and being excited about what the new year and years to come would bring.

While I was home, my mother sat an appointment to have my wisdom teeth removed before I went back to school. As a student-athlete, I was expected to return from break earlier than the other students because we had to practice. We were hosting a home conference game that Saturday, January 5th. Getting my teeth removed over break meant that I would have to return late. Following the extractions, I started running a fever. I communicated to my coach that I would return as soon as I was feeling better. There was not much concern other than when I was going to make it back. In college sports, there was no room for excuses. It was much different from high school. I was an athlete, and they were paying for my education therefore, whatever decision I made needed to be about the team first. Maybe they thought I was lying to extend my vacation, as a coach I probably would have thought the same thing but anyone who knows me knows I don't like to lie. I did not make it back to school until a day or two after I was supposed to be there. I was very sick by that time. On top of the fever, I was experiencing body aches and chills. I stayed in bed all day after I returned to the "bricks," which is what we called our housing unit on the small campus. I tried my best to nurse myself back to health because I knew we had practice early the next day.

Friday morning, when it was time for practice, I told my coach that I could not attend because I was too sick. This was unacceptable! The assistant coaches called me and told me I had to come to practice. I remember barely being able to walk, let alone run. I was very weak and could hardly breathe, but I had no choice. I had to practice, so I pushed myself. I remember feeling like I was going to die, my chest and throat were burning like never before. If my memory serves me correctly, we had practice again that same evening and a walk-through the next morning to prepare for our evening game.

On the day of the game, I was feeling a little better. With all the running during practice, I must have sweated out whatever I had come down with. I remember I did not sleep well the night before the game because the phone in the hall was ringing all night until one of my teammates took it off the hook. I stayed in bed most of the day until game time.

Before the game, I remember feeling extremely sad. For the first time since being away, I felt like I needed my family. I remember going into the coach's office and asking to use the phone to call home. My uncle answered the phone which was strange. Usually, my parents would answer or one of my brothers. It was not unusual for my uncle to be at the house because he would come over and play Dominoes with my dad, but he usually never answered the phone. When I asked to speak to my mom, he told me that my parents had gone to the store. I asked him if he was over at the house playing Dominoes and he said "yeah." Something about the way he sounded was off. I became suspicious. I thought he was hiding something from me. Then I became excited because I thought, what if my parents are surprising me and coming down to the school to see me play? I did not want to ruin the surprise, so I let him off the hook and got off the phone without asking more questions.

Before the game started, after pregame warm-ups were completed and the starting lineup was announced, I went to the bench and took a seat. As a freshman, I was not a starter and only played maybe 10-15 minutes a game. When I looked up towards the gym doors, I was shocked. Walking in the gym was about 15 of my family members. I remember locking eyes with my grandmother first. I was smiling from ear to ear, but she looked sad even though she tried to force a smile back at me. Looking back, I can see my grandmother's face vividly. I was so excited that I didn't give it much thought then.

I did not see my mom until just before halftime. I was too embarrassed to look back at everyone. Usually, by this time, I would have gotten into the game a few times. Now, for the first time, with all my family there, I was literally riding the bench. I became anxious, then embarrassed, then angry. I finally looked back and saw my mother who could tell that something was bothering me. She came down out of the bleachers to the bench. She asked if I was mad about the game. I told her "Yes," she said something to the extent of not worrying about the game, other stuff was more important and of course something about me going home. I dismissed that comment as usual because I thought she was just being mama, missing me, trying to protect me because I was clearly angry, and wanting me to come home.

If I had known I would not play, I could have told my family and saved them a trip. By this point, I was completely checked out. The game couldn't end fast enough. I became discouraged for the first time during my basketball career. It would not be the last time, but I did not know that something more important than basketball was about to change my life forever.

When the game was over and the coach delivered the post-game speech, I walked out of the locker room with tears in my eyes to go face my family. My father was standing outside of the doors. I hugged my dad and cried in his arms, letting all my emotions from the game go. My father hugged me and through my sobbing, I heard him say something about my brother, which baffled me. Why would he be talking about my brother when I'm upset about my game?

My brain was trying to put together what my father was talking about because he caught me off guard. I was not present. I wanted a minute to wallow in the most embarrassing thing that had ever happened to me. Quickly, my thoughts went back to home, to what I had left behind for the last five months. The dangers that were always present there. My feelings of embarrassment and anger were replaced with fear and anxiety. I managed to stop crying long enough to ask, "what brother?" My father stopped talking, now realizing that what I was crying about and what he thought I was crying about were not the same thing.

I looked up at my father's face through my teary eyes, he said, "Jamal." I asked him, "what happened to Jamal?" he didn't answer, I asked him again, "Daddy, what happened to Jamal?" My stomach dropped; my mind began racing. Jamal had problems with people from our old neighborhood. Those problems led to a lot of gunfire exchange and our old house being shot up. We moved away three years prior but maybe he ran into someone and this time they had shot him. Maybe there was a new beef with someone else that I wasn't aware of since being gone. How bad was it? Was he in the hospital? Would he be okay until we could all make it back home?

I remember the look on my father's face. It was the same look of sadness I saw in my grandmother's eyes a few hours ago. A mixture of sadness and pity. I could tell my dad was resistant to say what he had come all that way to tell me. He said, "Jamal died." I let out a yell that matched the pain of my soul tearing apart inside. I heard his words but could not comprehend how this had happened. My knees buckled below me, and I fell to the ground. My dad helped me up, and I saw my mother coming out of my coach's office. She must have been letting him know what happened, and that she had come to take me home. She walked back into the office and sat down on the couch. I ran after her and fell in her lap. I hugged her, but she was only a shell of herself. She just sat there. She did not cry. She had probably been doing that all day. She was there physically but my mother was not there mentally. Her mind was probably back home, on her son. She did not have enough strength to console me because she was trying to hold herself together. How can a mother ever wrap her mind around the unnatural pain of losing her child? Now, she was there to bring me home so I could be with my family.

After crying for what only seemed like a few seconds. I jumped up leaving my mother and ran into the locker room to retrieve my belongings. I did not say anything to my teammates. I felt them watching me, perplexed. I ran out of the locker-room down the hill to my dorm only to realize that I had forgotten my keys, so I ran back to the gym. When I entered the locker room this time, I saw my teammates crying, but at that moment I did not know why. I could not hear anything they said to me. By that time, the coach had delivered the news to everyone. I remember one, maybe more of my teammates hugging me. I broke away. I was on a mission to get back home, to get back to my brother. I felt like I could have run the entire three-hour trip back home to get to him. I told my teammates "I have to go", and I left. I ran out of the gym back to my room to pack so I could go home. My family picked me up at my dorm and we were on our way, not knowing if I would ever return. Not caring if I would return to school, to basketball, to my first love, to any of it. At that moment nothing mattered to me. I could not feel or think about anything except for pain. Brokenhearted, I cried the whole ride home.

I learned later; that in the wee hours of the morning my brother suffered cardiac arrest. A family member tried to call me to tell me about my brother's passing. They could not get through on the phone line that was off the hook from the night before. I am grateful that I did not have to be alone when I received the worst news of my life.

Eventually, I returned to school. I made that decision for my brother. After he died, I had an emptiness that led me to not care about anything, not even myself. No one and nothing seemed important. I was angry at the world and wanted to self-destruct. I had a battle going on inside my spirit. There was a side of me that wanted to allow the pain to take over and act out of my emotions. Then there was a side that was calling for me to still seek goodness, to still seek beauty, and to still be grateful. I had a comforter that was calling for me to lay this burden upon him. I did not know why. I did not want to, and I resisted that calling until I no longer could. I felt that losing my brother would be justification for messing up my life. My creator had other plans. He kept me. He touched my mind, and I used my gift to write out my emotions. When I wrote, it healed me, and eventually, my spirit changed. Instead of allowing my brother to be my excuse, he became my reason and everything I did was for him. I did not know my purpose or how to find it, so I made him my purpose. He would have been 23 years old on May 11th, 2002, but he did not live to see that day. I vowed to live the life that he did not have the chance to live.

I've loved, I've lost, I have experienced heartbreak many times. I have had close friends die unexpectedly. I have witnessed homicide on more than one occasion. I have had people walk away from me, or people that I cared about that I had to walk away from. I have given away pieces of my soul. I loved my brother with all my heart. I loved my friend Michelle in the purest of ways that friends can share. I've been in and fell out of what I thought was love a few times. I have learned how to live with the hurt and not allow it to kill me, but I thank God that he placed each one that I lost in my life because I learned how to live from them all.

Experiencing my greatest loss, taught me how precious life is. It taught me to love harder and to keep the ones that I love close. I learned to take every opportunity to let the people I love know how much I love and appreciate them. I do not have any regrets with anyone that I have lost because they all knew how I felt about them. The unexpected loss of my brother taught me most things that people take so seriously, really mean nothing. My "unbotheredness" at times, is not because I do not care about things but because it may not be the right thing to care about. I was told before that I move like the world is waiting on me. I know it is not, but I also know how fast time goes so I try my best to slow down and not take it for granted. I try not to forget to appreciate the small things. I want to appreciate the sun on my face and the butterflies in the grass. I want to appreciate the way the clouds move in the sky; I want to appreciate that I can walk, and think, and be, and be appreciative. One day all the things that we think are so important will fade away. Time is fleeting so I take time to appreciate time. I cherish the time that I share with those I care about. This is how I show gratitude.

What I learned about myself is that I am resilient. I have the same resilience that I see in my mother when she refuses to allow life to break her. The resilience that drove her to return to school at the age of 56 to accomplish her dreams of obtaining her diploma. I have the resilience I see in my grandmother who was born without a hip. Her whole life she was told what she could not do because of her handicap but she defied all the odds. The same resilience is in me that I have seen in my granny, who was a maid that worked in mansions nursing and raising white children. The resilience that I have heard in stories about my paternal great-great-grandmother, who was a slave but fought against her slave owner and fled captivity. That resilience lives within me. It is in my DNA. This is the same resilience I've tapped into, fighting to not allow my broken heartedness to kill me. My resilience drives me to be the best version of myself. I want to make my brother proud because I know he is in my cloud of witnesses. Whenever in life I cannot find the motivation to do things for myself, I do it for him. I do it for our children, our nieces, and our nephews. I do it so that I can inspire them to live the life that my brother could not.

I have written many poems about my brother over the years but being true to character, I have rarely spoken about how his loss affected me. I was around so many others who were dealing with their brokenness that mine never seemed significant enough to talk about. So, I made my role to be the strong one. I was the one people came to when they needed a listening ear, or advice on how to heal. I was the fixer and yet for a long time, I never tried to fix myself. I allowed things to live inside of me until they festered and stunk. Telling myself that I was strong, and I was okay when I was not. I was so wrapped up in surviving that I did not know that I was not okay. What I know now is even strong people need a shoulder to lean on sometimes. Admitting when you need help does not make you weak. It is a sign of strength and wisdom. There is nothing brave about remaining broken.

Unfortunately, I believe that heartbreak is inevitable. As long as I am living there is a great possibility that I will experience more heartbreak. Knowing this, I work daily to build myself up mentally, emotionally, and spiritually so that I am equipped to address heartbreak when it happens again.

The After Effect
(OF A BROKEN HEART)

Can't eat, restless sleep
Body shaking and trembling,
Nerves bad, welt marks,
Face looking sad.

Nappy head, lay in bed,
Same thoughts running through my mind.
Bad thoughts,
Who's at fault? Feels like wasted time.

Throat thick, can't breathe,
Feel sick, can't leave,

Tears fall, stomach crawls,
Feel weak, can't speak
Voice squeaks,

Deep breaths,
Heavy chest,

Heart hurts,
Soul shakes, spirit breaks,

Red eyes, tear stains,

Headache,
Runny nose,
Story goes…

Regroup,
Headstrong,
Reminisce,
Move on!

Jamal

So many thoughts running thru my mind
It's hard to keep focus
So, I dissect them one at a time.

I lost my brother
I need a friend
I miss my family
I want a companion

It's hard on me
I'll say it again.

Memories flood my mind
Hard to concentrate
On schoolwork
When your heart aches.

I wanna go home
I wanna quit
I must go on
I can't handle it

Missing the love of people who understand
Lost a friend because he wants to be my man
Been in love before
Don't wanna open that door again.

I'm getting tired
I'm getting weak
I write words so my soul can speak

New problems
New pressures
Things just don't make sense
Plead insanity as my defense.

I can't breathe
I'm suffocating
I try to be strong
I carry on

My soul shakes
In a state of confusion,
I try to win
I feel like I'm losing.

My sanity
My sanctuary
My mind
My privacy
My thoughts
My sense of being.

Things seem so petty
Cause
"Nothing Even Matters…at all,"
But Love.

I put things in perspective because I am blessed
Plagued with confusion
Unsure about what my path holds next
But I have faith
The sun will surely shine
I lost my brother
My soul is crying

Lie to Me

Tell me what I want to hear
let's not deal with what's real
don't want to face the reality
there are no consequences in fantasies
just another happily ever after
but in reality
comes tears after laughter

Yeah, tell me you love me
because it's easy for me to be carried away in your words
and interpret your actions as I see fit
yes, you love me
just,
tell me this
because no…I've never met anyone that
was comparable
but if you happened to express the truth
it may render too unbearable

Tell me you want me to be your wife
because it sounds better than "baby mama"
and I'm not sure if I even want to be

but I would have a little more dignity
by telling people I was your Wifey

Tell me that you want only me
so that I won't have to deal with the reality
that I have accepted sharing because I can't stand to be
alone

Tell me that I'm your one and only
when you're in a relationship with some other chick
but you "really don't want to be," and
I will believe that shit
even though my commonsense
can't seem to comprehend
how someone can stay in a situation
that they "really don't want to be in,"

For over 3 years
without any kids
and unraveling strings attached
go-ahead, please
tell me that

I can't hold you accountable
to the truth when I'm
lying to myself
I keep trying,
inside I'm dying
and crying out to myself
"Baby girl, you have to love you
before you can love anybody else!"

Later, I'll regret that
I am not yet at
the point where I'm ready to accept
the truth
so, for now
I'll allow
you to
keep
lying to me.

Just a Thought

Why do I always have to be the one to give?
Give up
Give in

I'm trying to let go
Let out
Cry out, cry inside
Until a whimper becomes a whisper
And I can breathe again

Breathe out
Breathe in
Be in unison

With how precious I am
Instead of what you may want or need
Until my heart no longer bleeds

Until I accept
That I, you will never need
I, you will never see
Mine, you will never be

Be one with, grow and become with
If we are meant to be then it shall be
Definitely

I mustn't forget that you are who you are unapologetically
Wishing that our worlds could play out like a fantasy
Romantically

However, the reality of the situation is that
You've been letting me go
Forgetting me slow

What can I do to make you notice me?
Make you grab me tight and never let go of me?
Make you want to put a stronghold on me
And when it's time to let go
Hope, I can walk around nobly

Hmm...

...Just a thought

I Cried for You Last Night

Every time I laid my head down on my pillow
Emotions came over me
Before I knew it tears gathered in my eyes
Something came over me…

The realization that
I will never see you again
Suddenly, rushed over me

When do I stop grieving?

When does the hurt go away?
Or are these unsuspected tears here to stay?
Far and in-between
Or
Every-other-day!

Some tears were because I feel like
I never got to know you
Like I never got a chance to meet my
Best friend
That I know you would have been

The closest person to me…
Maybe you were…but before I can remember
Maybe you always were…

I feel that you still
Watch over me
Are still protecting me
Still carrying me

I can't help but wish
That we could take family trips
Or celebrate our birthdays together

See that smile on your face
And have you there to celebrate all
These important times together

Wonder how you would make my life different
Not understanding why, you had to go away

Can't help but feel like it's not fair that you're not here

Never forgotten
Deeply missed
A missing link in our chain
And right now, there's no way for me to hold it together

Wondering what you would be doing
With yourself if you had the chance to live
Wondering if you would have had more kids
Wondering if you too were a sacrificial lamb

Now I can't allow your life to be given in vain
Don't know why I feel like it's my responsibility
To carry that load but
I won't complain

I can take it

Mama said she felt like you were the one that got the least
When it came to material things
It surely wasn't because love was lost on you

That made me wonder how you felt
growing up
What were your inner struggles?
What were your deepest thoughts?
Your feelings?

Wish we had time for me to be
The one you would call to get advice from
Wondering who
You had to talk to about life

Wish that I could have been
Your friend
Hopefully, we'll get that chance again

In the hereafter

(I love you bro, love sis)

PART III

Love

Love: The Ultimate Sacrifice

I love, love. Love is the most beautiful, most complex, most fulfilling emotion that I have ever experienced. My understanding of love has expanded as I've grown as an individual. Love pushes me the most to grow, even more than my heartbreak or struggles. It is not the pain of losing my brother that drives me to want to be great. It is the love that I have for him and the love that he had for me. His love wanted me to be great, my love wants to be great for him. Love challenges everything that I think. Love made me worthy. It is the most essential factor in every choice that I make.

My most important roles are those of mother and spouse. Having a healthy, loving relationship teaches me how to be deserving of love. My Rosebud taught me what love looks like when it is reciprocated. I've learned what it is like for a companion to accept and love my weaknesses. True love lets me know it is okay to put myself fully into something good. Love allows a safe place for me to let down my guard and be vulnerable. It teaches me how to accept and expect goodness in my life. Initially, I was not good at love. I had unrealistic expectations. It took me ten years to figure out how to coexist in a relationship without trying to make it fit into my preconceived ideas about what I thought it should be. I looked to my spouse to make me happy. This was impossible. The more they tried, the more I required. Only by learning the true meaning of love, and remembering how to love myself, was I then able to show up as a better partner.

Being a mother teaches me patience, it teaches me not to take life so seriously all the time and to take time to enjoy the moment. Motherhood forces me to make space to look at life through an innocent and inquisitive lens, forcing me to view life from a new standpoint. Motherhood reinforces the importance of being the example and holding myself accountable. I do not take this assignment lightly. Both relationships teach me to trust and the importance of effective communication. I want to be a better listener, I have not mastered it, but I am working on it daily.

Many people only love who they think you are or who they want you to be. Few people truly know what it means to love unconditionally. Those that I love are the people that know my failures, my weaknesses, my shortcomings, and all the things that make me flawed, yet they choose to love me as I am. They love me without judgement. They don't try to change me or fix me to fit into a person they deem worthy to love. They don't wish me to be something or someone different.

I love my friends like I love my family. The words love and friend are, in my opinion, frequently misused. I do not say "I love you" carelessly and I do not call everyone my friend. To be a friend is a responsibility. It is an obligation that requires work and effort as any relationship.

The people who have hurt me the most are those who were close to me. People that I least expected. When good things happened in my life that allowed me to be honored, I noticed the people I thought would be happy for me weren't.

When I achieved goals I worked hard for, they would try to minimize my accomplishments. I would say that those people really didn't love me, but I believe that Judas really did love Jesus. The challenge is learning how to love those who may not show you love how you need them to. As I am learning how to operate in love, I learned it is possible to identify my Judas and still show them grace. However, this does not mean that you should continue to interact and allow those individuals access to you.

You may have to love some people from a distance because everyone you love or that loves you, are not equipped to go on your journey. I choose to surround myself with people who respect me, and respect who I am called to be. I choose those who gently give me correction when needed because I believe this is also love. I choose those that encourage me to follow my dreams. I cannot be aligned with individuals who hinder my growth. Maya Angelou said, "if you love someone, liberate them." Sometimes those you love are intentionally or inadvertently used to deter you from your purpose. Some people are not on your level spiritually, emotionally, or mentally. You must know where to place these people in your life or if they deserve a place there at all. I am very selective and am extremely loyal to those that I have found to embody the qualities of a friend. The few that I call friends, I love deeply and wholeheartedly.

If you ask my grandmother who is now 81 years old, she will tell you she and her oldest friend have been sister-friends since first grade. They've loved each other for a lifetime. My grandmother told me she never tells her friends what they should do with their lives, she would only tell them if it were her, what she would do. I've taken that advice so that I can work on being a better friend. If we happen to have different opinions about the world, I will try to see it from your angle but respect my opinion without being offended or trying to change it. Allow us to agree to disagree.

I've learned how to be okay with walking away from dead connections and negative relationships. I had to become comfortable in knowing that everyone does not show love the same way and if the relationship does not work out, not to take it personally. I have heard recently that a lot of times we stay connected to people that we share a history with. I want to connect with people who can also share with me in my future and I in theirs. I want to stay in a relationship with people who can support my strengths and vice versa. I want to keep my friends close who encourage me to be my best self and push me to greatness. I want to hold on to connections that inspire me to elevate in life. My goal is to reciprocate love with those who show me they love me.

I have learned to be reasonable in my expectations of others. Empty words no longer excite me. Do not profess to love me but never show love in your actions. If I love you, you have a friend in me for life; A trustworthy, loyal, loving, silly, supportive, encouraging friend. A listening ear, a word of advice, a prayer warrior, a truthful perspective, or a Thelma to your Louise. Those close to me know this and are the same to me in return. They understand why I love hard, and honestly because I've shared my heart. They know that I always have the best of intentions, but I am not perfect. I am striving always for perfection, and they do not discourage me from working towards greatness. I forgive easy but I never forget and when I am tired, I simply walk away. As I continue to grow in love, I look forward to being a better mother, a better spouse, a better daughter, a better friend, and an all-around better person.

$\mathcal{D}ear\ \mathcal{S}on$

Son, the fear that I feel is real.
You have yet to learn of
George Floyd, Trayvon Martin, Tamir Rice, or Emmit Till.

I don't mean to project,
It's just that it would kill me if I let
You step out into this world unprotected.

Understand that you are an endangered species.

Your appearance must be immaculate. Please son,
Take that hoodie off your head and
Pull up your pants.

I want the best image of you to be projected,
When you walk out of our door, you are subjected
To their perception.

You are intelligent, yes,
But they won't see or hear that.
They will not ask before they shoot
If you make all As and Bs in school.

No, it's not fair.
Believe me, I understand.
But listen to what I'm saying,
They will not wait to confirm that it's just a cellphone in
your hand.

You,
rather your brown hue
Is a threat to them.

Yes, God did make you beautiful and in the likeness of him,
Even still, instead of seeing you as a king
You're just another black boy to them.

They won't know that before we eat dinner, you lead grace.
That you pray for your family before you go to bed at night,
That you are gentle and would rather play than to fight.

We don't want you to coward down.
Always be a man, show respect,
Look them in the eye, speak clear,

But keep both hands on the wheel
And control your emotions.

We teach you to strive for perfection
because statistics have shown,
That you will not receive their grace
If you make a mistake.

It breaks my heart to have to teach you this
We just,
Want you to make it home safely.

God as my witness
If something ever happened to you
He would also have to take me.

No matter how old you get
You'll always be our baby

Even so, I know that
One day we'll have to let you go.
I've been praying over you since the womb,
Asking God to provide
Protection over you.

Expressing my love for you
But always knowing that you are not mine,
You are HIS

My love keeps me laying hands on you while you sleep,
Praying over you at night.
My love for you is why I tell you no,
My "no's," are not to restrict but to protect.

My Love for you is why I will always tell you the truth.
My Love will always want the best for you
Even if that means that you are not happy with my decision.

I don't take my role lightly.
My role is to raise you to be a man,
Hopefully, if you choose to be…, somebody's husband.
So, I will always protect you!

With all my love,
Mommy

Never Again, Once More

A beautiful specimen of a human
Afraid to love you yet here I stand,
Waiting but not quite willing
To totally commit to the feeling
Not allowing myself to open up and believe
Not quite sure if I'm ready to receive
But yet, for some reason, your words I believe
Mad at myself because I'm feeling so weak
Feeling like at any moment I may surrender in defeat
And all this is happening so unexpectedly
Telling myself to walk away maybe regretfully
Not supposed to be ready to love again…
Allegedly
But you have persistently showed me your feelings
Unforgettably
I shouldn't have let you get so close to me
Giving you an opportunity
And exposing me
To how my world is supposed to be
I must admit I became tempted
To learn more,

Nosily
While subconsciously allowing you to know the inner me
No longer am I looking at love as if it's an enemy
But that wasn't your intention…
Supposedly
…or was it???
Was that how you got me to ease down my guard
By catching me off guard
Soften me up where you knew I was hard
Work on my soul until I gave you my heart
Where those your intentions from the start??? Slick bastard
(smiling)
Slowly tear down my walls,
Rip my distrust apart
You're asking for disaster
Urging you to stay emotionally unattached
Warning you to walk away now and don't look back
I can see that your hard-headed
Don't want you to give in
To your feelings
Because you might live to regret it
Your refusal to believe
That I can't give you what you need
Was proven when you said you see
Something in me,
That I don't see
And you were willing
To explore it
That you would prove to me, that you are here for it
So, as we moved forward
I begin to give in

Reluctantly
With a warning to you that it will not be easy
I guess even though I said never again
Once more
I find myself willing
to give in
To love again

Rosebud

You believe in giving your love with all loyalty

As if it is your duty
Come spoil me

To get used to honesty and integrity
How dare me?...

Put my trust in you as if you could never hurt me

To do that would be saying that you
could make no mistakes
I couldn't put such a burden on you
for our relationship's sake

But for my heart's sake
I can't help but imagine

That I could place you somewhere in my life
After God
But before myself if only by a fraction

Or that yourself and myself
Could dwell in the same domain

That ourselves as a unit
Could be blessed in Jesus' name

That my joy
Could share your joy
And my pain could share your pain

That your and my heart could beat one and the same
That there
Could be a possibility that we could share
the same last name

You spark my senses
Since this
Game at times can seem so senseless

I gravitate to your energy
In hopes that you receive me

Restore me

Your eyes, your touch, your spirit
Has lured me

Floored me

Hoping that my words don't come off empty
You simply
Tempt me

Impress me with your humor
Caress me with your intellect

My only regret
Is that
We didn't let
This magic
Happen sooner

Keep me on my toes
With your wit
I suppose

At times I stare at you, in awe
Why was it I
You chose?

It's unreal to me how in sync we are
Like my thoughts are yours
Trying to be on that vibe
Like what's mine is yours

Wish that we could pick a time in this place
A corner out in space
That we could claim as ours

The sun, the moon, the stars
Become jealous of the glow you give me
Hard to explain this feeling
That is within me

Send me
On a journey
In search of our future together
In hopes that I might feel this way
Forever

You're spinning me into delusional imageries

Yeah, I know it's silly
But that's just the romantic in me

I'm hopeless
I hope this
Doesn't sound like a bunch of words with no focus

Not a proposal or declaration of love just
Feelings, thoughts, and emotions
In random order being expressed

No more
No less
Just

Take it as it is cause I've already seen our future
Me as your wife
A house, and dog
And our two kids

Thinking back to the beginning
Where I don't know who you is
Just an introduction
By a mutual friend

This begins
With a handshake
A smile
A glance

Leading to where we are now and
hopes of where we will be then

Support System

I need someone that is strong enough to support me,

My personality
My weight
My trauma
My past
My flaws
My moods
My insecurities
My success

All the things that make me, me

My needs
My wants
My anxiety
My thoughts
My fears
My triumphs
My joy
My tears

My spirituality
My dreams
My depression
My reality
My Love

You Are

You Are my Word, my Prophecy
A Godsend
Sent here for me
You don't judge me
You unconditionally love me
You are of me,

You are words that I can't speak
You are so many things to me
All that I wish to be
You amaze me

You are my knowledge
You are my power and strength

You are my common sense
You are my intelligence.
I adore you
I cherish you

No one can compare to you
I hope to be there for you
Like you are there for me

You are beyond my love
Cause people fall out of that
You are beyond feelings and even words you just are

And we are
Spiritually together
This bond can never be severed.
I call on you religiously.
And you answer my prayers

You are the answer to my riddle.
The beginning to my end
My sweetest Sin
So then, I repent
And do it all over again

You are,
You are!
You are.

PART IV

Evolution

Evolution: Growing Pains

I have spent a lot of time learning life lessons. Some lessons I learned by observing others and some I learned while making my own mistakes. I've often wished that I did not have to go through some of the growing pains that I have. I know without the lesson I would have missed the blessing that came after. The journey is difficult, but I am determined to take what I have learned and allow myself to evolve into a better person.

There was a period that I got into fights almost every summer. The irony is that I've always desired peace. I never wanted to fight, I just bought into the notion that I had to. I have watched people around me who did not have the proper tools to handle conflict. I watched how they would lose control and I also witnessed the regret that followed. I did not want to repeat the pattern. I had the foresight to know the outcome of losing control would not be favorable. At times it was hard to maintain that control, so I became what I never wanted to be. A person who did not have control over my emotions. A person whose emotions had control over me. When wrath is unleashed, it usually can't be tamed and can lead to destruction. It is much like Bruce Banner trying to control the Hulk. I have had those times and I am thankful that God kept me. A few people are walking around who have no clue they were saved by grace.

I never was the type of person who started any trouble, but I never backed down either. I think if anything I mislead people or gave them a false sense of security. If someone approached me with conflict, most of the time I was quiet. I might even laugh because it was entertaining. I have never been witty or quick with words, so I do not argue. I just remember what my mama told me. "Let em talk until their blue in the face, but if they put their hands on you, you better try to knock their head off their shoulders."

I remember being so bottled up that it scared me to get into physical altercations. Not scared for myself but scared for the other person because a part of me wanted an excuse to completely lose it. I remember telling a friend that I was scared to lose it because I thought I may snap and try to kill someone. I had kept so many things bottled up inside of me. I did not think I could stop myself if things ever escalated to the point of getting physical. Hearing my mother say "let people talk until they're blue in the face" helped me to be slow to react when people tried to use their words against me.

In hindsight, sometimes I let people get away with too much. I was either unbothered or quiet sitting on ready. When I was quiet during conflict a storm would be brewing on the inside. I did not have the skills yet to articulate what was going on, so I went from being unbothered to shutting down. When I was in shut down mode, there was no reasoning, just trapped emotions. Since I was not good with verbal warfare, I became frustrated with my lack of response. I did not have the quick thinking to respond and people's trash-talking annoyed me. My thought was we were either going to be cool, which I preferred, or we were going to throw hands, either way was fine with me. Arguing and trying to "front" was a waste of my time. When someone continued to talk trash, I would become angry at feeling disrespected. Still quiet, I often continued to let people talk until I became so angry and bothered that I would unleash the Hulk. Many times, thank God, there was someone there to deescalate. To those on the outside, it either appeared that I was afraid and did not defend myself. When I reached the point of losing it, it may have appeared that I went from being unbothered to overreacting. The funny thing is I would have felt worse and been disappointed in myself if I had lost it. Most of the time the person's issue had nothing to do with me. Their actions were their way of feeding their ego. I've always had the ability to recognize that.

The schools in our neighborhood were not the best so my mom would always send me where she thought I could have the most success. For a time, I used my grandmother's address to attend a better school. This meant that the bus would drop me off at my grandmother's home until my parents could pick me up. At the time I did not hang with a clique. I'd listened to my mother's warnings about the trouble that hanging and gossiping with a bunch of girls could cause. I never knew that I was also a target because I was by myself at a time when being in a clique was the thing to do. Females always felt like they had something to prove. I was never pressed or impressed.

I knew that the girls on this block were known for jumping people, so I always kept my distance. I didn't consider any of them to be a friend, but I was cordial with everyone. On this day, the vibe was different. I have always had a gift to read a room. Now I know that gift is called discernment, so when the energy changed, I felt it. Guys who usually would talk to me were giving me the head nod.

No one was making eye contact. Normally, I'm included in the conversation but now everyone was whispering around me. The females went from being fake cool to behaving in a way that let me know there was some tension. After I got off the bus I went into my grandmother's house and put a kitchen knife in my pocket. I didn't start trouble, but I didn't back down either. I had to go to school so I would have to face them, eventually. My thinking was we might as well get it over with. There were at least four girls, so I figured my weapon evened the playing field. When I went back outside, they were ready to fight. Heavy coats started coming off and girls were putting on gloves and skull caps. What they did not know was that I was ready as well. As they approached me, one guy from their hood stepped in between us and stopped anything from happening. He had shown interest in me, and we had been communicating. Obviously, he knew they planned to jump me that day, I just didn't know if it was his idea or theirs. Afterward, I questioned if his interest was genuine or if that was a ploy to set me up. Maybe he just lost the guts to go through with it or figured I was a nice enough person that he didn't want to watch what was about to go down? That is how things went in the hood. I was one decision away from jeopardizing my life, but I was ready to do what I felt I needed to do to protect myself.

I always had a fear of God. As I said before, I never wanted to be the type of person who started trouble or bullied people because I felt I would be punished. When things like this happened, it caused me to want to do bad things to people who I felt wronged me. I had not done anything to those girls. It was all about trying to show off, and for what? That pissed me off! I had all kinds of thoughts and feelings. I thought, I could just catch them all by themselves, one-on-one to have a fair fight, or I could just walk up to the toughest one and punch her in the face. Maybe that would send the others a message that they should think twice about messing with me. My mama told me stories about girls getting jumped and being cut in the face with razors. I didn't put that past these hood rats so I knew I couldn't allow that to happen. Because I am a thinker, I tried to stay 10 steps ahead of any situation, so I thought about different scenarios just in case. It upset me that people thought they could test me. It also upset me that I was put in a situation where I had to defend myself. If I told my mom she would just confront them, and I didn't want people thinking that I needed my mommy to fight my battles. What was I supposed to do?

After that situation, I operated differently. I sat in the front of the bus so I could see who was getting on and would watch them in the mirror above the driver. I made sure I was the first one off the bus so that I wouldn't step off into an ambush. I carried a knife in my backpack for a while and was always on alert. That was exhausting. When you're constantly in survival mode, it takes a toll on you. Luckily, I made it through the school year without incident.

One thing I did to find some peace besides writing was listen to music. I really enjoyed R&B music. It seemed to do the trick to calm the beast inside. When I heard Mary J. Blige sing it moved me. Listening to Mary was like having a best friend who understood everything that I was going through in my life. I could tell that she understood my struggles I coped with the anger, pain, and confusion by covering it up because I didn't know how to release it. I listened to Mary speak about the pain that I felt. I would turn the music up to drown out my tears or I would let them fall on the paper as I wrote.

After many years I began working on myself. The fight inside of me evolved. I no longer wanted to give anyone the ability to push the buttons that controlled my emotions. I had become used to drama. In the place that I am in my life today, I have no time for drama or people who dwell in that space. I still have a fighting spirit but now I fight for my dreams, my peace, and my sanity. I pray for people who are still where I once was mentally and emotionally. I no longer cover up pain and trauma, I address it so that I can heal. I do not just fight for myself; I also fight for others when I see that they have not yet found their voice.

A Common Misconception

A common misconception
Derived from your perception
Never seen as the exception
Labeled "common" at your discretion

Do you still see me to be naïve?
Being without nobility
Catering gullibly
To your needs

Hmm

What a shame of the things
That were once not known
But like Maya Angelou
I too know of the caged bird's song

So, thank God for my evolution
Which brought forth the resolution
This is a common misconception
Derived from your perception

You wonder, why I am not angered by what you
Perceive me to be?
Although others may think I should be
I graciously "thank you"
For putting up a picture of the person that you see

And I'll stand tall
While looking down on how
Short your realities fall

Pictured me as weak
No, my dear
Not at all

It's a shame that you take my kindness
For weakness
Only because you're used to people
Who are full of BS
So, when someone real comes
into your view
You don't know what to do

I no longer care about what others perceive me to be
I don't have time to try,
Won't be inauthentic to myself, pretending I am, what I'm not
Patience for your ignorance has been a challenge
But I tried

I can't, I won't, no more
I have so much that I have been called to live for
I cannot continue to apologize that you don't see
Everything that you too were called to be

No longer will I shrink for you
I am no longer synced with you
Can't sink with you

But I love you, the love has just changed
As I pray that you go on to bigger and better things
Because I am
I'm sure that you did not expect this maturity from me
As you realize now that I have never been
The person that you have perceived

Not Satisfied

I'm not satisfied where I am in my life
But I'm thankful that I'm not where I could have been,
I'm thankful because I will not become complacent
Always reaching and searching for more
Looking for opened windows and unlocked doors
Thankful to be blessed, yet I always want more
Until I have enough
Not just enough
But all that I need
God said he will supply my every need

I ask him to allow my cup to overflow
And that to which I am ignorant
Give me knowledge that I can know
And those places that I have not traveled give me courage
that I may go
And all that I am not now, give me guidance that I may be so

I'm no longer what I used to be but not yet what I am to become
Believe that I am on the right path
Just look at how far I've come

Know that God is all-powerful for I praise him for where
he's brought me from
Forever my trials will serve as a testament to the miracles
that he has done

I'm not satisfied because I know that this is not all he has
in store for me
So, I'll pray for patience until I get to where he wants me to be.

Then and Now

Don't look at me and see
Who I used to be,
That would be ignorant of you
And unfair to me

To do so
Is to insinuate that I have no capability to grow,
When, the way that my life has changed
You really do not know

Do you not take the time to hear
The change in the topic of my speech?
Things that I once thought important
Now hold no relevance to me.

Some of the things that I used to do
I no longer do anymore,
The way that I act
Is no longer like that
My whole mind-track
Has matured.

Do you feel that you're able to change?
…If you are, then why not I?

Where my strength is in acknowledging my weaknesses,
Your weakness can't understand why.

I've been through things that changed
My heart
And have opened my eyes,
If you took the time to realize
You may walk away surprised.

Don't judge me by how I used to be
Cause everyone must grow,
Just take the time to get to know my mind
And the new me you might get to know.

Some things I changed in Jesus's name
Some things were changed through life,
Some things were just by common sense
And some things were so my soul could live right.

Then, I never guarded myself against the world
I allowed my feelings to show,
Never knowing that users would use it against me
Because I left myself too exposed.

Then, I would be hurt
When they wanted to walk away,
Now, if they go, I let them go
The one's who want to will stay.

Then, I was more concerned with how others felt
So, I pushed my feeling aside,
Now, I love myself too much
To allow them to destroy my pride.

Then, I allowed jealousy and insecurities to dwell deep within me,
Now, I've replaced those with self-assurance and confidence and my footstools are my enemies.

Then, I cared about what people thought about me
So, people, I tried to impress,
Now, If I got it, I got it
If I don't, I don't
I can give you no more, no less.

I didn't wise up overnight
I've changed over time, steady and slow,
The person I am now, you will not know
If you refuse to let my past go.

Ask yourself if you can value the ME
I am to be,
If not, then you should go
Out of my life for this friendship can no longer be so.

Love Letter to Myself

I'm a bleeding heart for ya baby
My heart has been ripped and torn into so many pieces
I wasn't sure if there were any emotions left for ya baby

Dripping tears and fears of built-up heartbreak
Heartache is no stranger to me
So, I just learned how to put phrases upon pages
Used as a compass to map out my pain
At different stages

Used as a universal language to all races and ages
Cause you're never too young to love
Nor too old to hurt

Always the right age
To learn lessons
Every day is a test when
Often, I felt distressed and

The pain that was inflicted upon me never made it any better
Never eased my conscious
So, I began to write this love letter

It said…
"Get in touch with your feelings for you
Everyone isn't safe to give your heart to
It's okay to be greedy and take some time for you

You will make some mistakes but that's okay
Learn to forgive yourself,
You'll always have God
Even when it feels that you don't have anyone else

Give yourself permission to cry
It only cleanses the pain inside

Believe in yourself,
Never seek validation from anybody else

Accept correction,
Seek wisdom and truth
And don't be afraid to show others the beauty that is within you."

Truth

Someone once told me "Just tell me the truth"
As I opened my mouth to let them have it…
I didn't
It felt like an explanation would be way too long-winded

But that didn't stop my mind from racing and what it
said was
"You wouldn't recognize the truth if it smacked you in the face"
You see, the truth is what many claim to want but
Once you give it to them, they don't know what to do with it

The truth is what real people deal with and fake people run
from
I've been dealing with truth my whole life
I survive off Truth
Pick my friends through Truth
You slipped through because I didn't consult Truth about you

You lack truth which means you lack realness
So why would I continue to waste my valuable time
With someone who is just a facade?

I mean really, that would be silly
The truth is, "silly" just isn't me,
That fake s--- I can't deal with
That just isn't Free

What makes me so real? you ask…
Well, I consulted the Truth about me, and
He showed me the truth about Thee
And at first, I judge it, then I hated it, then I accepted it,
then I loved it

He showed me the truth about why I was raised in the projects
Witnessed a man die right before my eyes
Then concealed drugs in my pockets all by the age of six

He showed me the truth about why my life was threatened
by gun violence
And why I suffered the pain of losing my brother
It isn't that it happened it's that I survived it

As this was revealed I learned the truth about me
That I am necessary

Truth said to me,
My child, you will endure pain for a while, but you'll come
out victorious.
I'll place you before a pedestal to speak words of truth about
life and about struggle

And you'll deliver my lost children back unto me through
your words
I'll use your words as a ministry, use your words my daughter
to speak
And speak truth

Tell my daughters that they are beautiful young women,
And that they don't have to accept less than the best from
a man,
They shall carry themselves as the queens that they are
within,
The queens that I have made them. I'm preparing the king
who loves me
To be a man who can lead them, so tell her just be patient

Speak peace among your friends, encourage them and celebrate
Show that it's a lie to say it's only competition among women
And female friendships are full of hate
As you speak words of truth all of you shall be great

Only allow conversations that are good
And even though you are the only girl born onto your parents
I'll provide you a sisterhood

Speak life into young men and uplift your young brothers
Encourage them to love one another
Tell them stories of your nephew and your brother
You'll connect with them, and they'll be able to feel your real

The devil will try to stop you from speaking my truth with
a trick called anxiety

But rely on me, keep your eyes on me
And I'll bring you through it every time
I'll provide you with peace of mind
This is your assignment
The Truth shall not be silenced

The violence that you have witnessed has prepared you
To stand strong on solid ground and not be shaken
When the storm is raging, and someone tells you that they
can no longer stand it
You are the chosen one to bear witness and speak of a peace
that surpasses all understanding

He told me to tell the truth about how I feel
Because some people need to heal
That are struggling with grief,
He told me that when I put words to my tears
That it will mend hearts when I speak

He said He's seen that I've gained compassion from not
having
So, because I've remained humble, He'll give me more than
I could ever ask for
That I will have a testimony about everything that I've
endured

Everything that I live for shall be blessed
All I have to do
Is remain focused on who
I am and whose I am
Because I am living proof
Of the manifestation of living in Truth.

PART V

Self

Self: Know Thy Self

The journey of getting to know your inner self must be intentional. It is a lifelong process as we live and grow. Sometimes you may not like what you discover but it is necessary to grow. Bishop T.D. Jakes said, "the way you grow once you are grown is not in your body, it's in your head". During my process of seeking who I am meant to be, I had to forsake all others and be selfish to get from the Almighty exactly what I needed. What only HE could give me. What I already had, but just needed to uncover. HE showed me who I was NOT, and those were great lessons. They hurt but were necessary for my growth. In the times that I felt like I was taking steps backward, I was steadily moving forward slowly. I work on myself each day. I have not reached my full potential, but I believe I am on the right path now that I have the tools that I need.

I remember being about five years old when I was called a "bitch" for the first time by the one person who was never supposed to hurt me. Around the age of 10, I was called "fast" because I was dancing in the front yard. I remember being called a "trick" and "whore" when I was only about 11 or 12 even though I held on to my purity longer than anybody that I knew. I remember talking to my cousin and crying and laughing at the same time because of how hurt and confused I was. In my innocence, I did not understand what of my behavior made me deserve to be called these names. Even though they made me cry, I was very clear that those names did not define me. Something deep down inside allowed me to turn being called those names into motivation to be better than what they said I was. Most of these labels came from adults who I now understand did not receive what they needed from adults when they were kids. Being called these names taught me to put little weight on what someone else speaks upon you, especially when it is not positive. At the time I did not know myself, so I could have allowed those labels to shape who I was going to become. As an adult, I try to be very careful with my words. I do not allow negative talk or gossip into my conversations. I try to take every chance that I get to acknowledge people when they are doing something good. I don't want to use my words as weapons, rather tools to speak life into people.

Still today, I hate when someone tries to put labels or limits on me. I do not like to be placed in a box. I am very careful not to do that to others. People are too complex to be made out to be just one thing, or one way. I am also cognitive about what words I use when I speak to and around children. My great-grandmother, Vivian Conway, used to say not to call babies "bad". I understand that now because words matter. It is my responsibility to use my words to empower and encourage others. No person on this Earth knows what you are called to be, only God can reveal that to you. I would never want to cause someone not to reach their full potential because of something that I said.

After my first year of college, I returned home with no scholarship, no job, and no plans for school. I felt like I was just floating through life. I had no direction, nor did I have a vision of what my next move should be. I think at some point I may have stopped caring and became numb. I experimented with smoking weed. I started partying more and more, and I became careless with myself, exploring my sexuality and having meaningless encounters. After my brother died, I dove into a relationship seeking to fill a void. That relationship caused me heartbreak because I showed up as a broken person, I did not know or care about my self-worth.

One day, in the summer before my sophomore year, I received an unexpected phone call from a local female basketball star. She was going on a full ride to play basketball at a Division I University. I had played with and against her in high school. I always admired her skills from a distance, but we weren't close friends, so I was surprised when she called me. A coach from a local community college where she'd played the last two years, saw me play in a summer league game and asked her to call me. He wanted to know what my plans were for playing basketball again.

When I got that call, my life was at a standstill. I was working at a truck rental company and attending night school classes, while dealing with residual feelings from a dead relationship. That phone call changed my life. It gave me hope to plan for tomorrow. Then, the day before I would have signed my scholarship, I found out I was pregnant. My world was turned upside down yet again. This time it was by my doing. In my carelessness, I'd received an unintentional consequence. All I could think of was how I would become a statistic. The very thing that I never wanted to be. I thought about how I did not have an education and was living in my parent's home with no means to raise a child. When I let my ex know the situation the only thing they asked was "so what you going to do?" There was no support from that end, we did not even live in the same state. I thought about how disappointed everyone would be. In my 19-year-old mind, there was no way that I could go to school and play basketball while raising a child so I made a choice, a choice that I would regret for the rest of my life. I chose not to go forward with the pregnancy.

I only told three people about the pregnancy. Of course, the other person who shared the responsibility for my condition, and two women that I considered being like sisters to me. One was stern about this not being a situation that I should ever get myself into again. She let me know she loved me and would be there for me through my decision. The other called me a "murderer." She turned her back on me and threatened to tell everyone. I understood her disappointment. As much as she hated my decision, so did I. No one was as disappointed in me as I was in myself. All my life I had fought to overcome adversity, I was unmovable in my will and determination to be better and to achieve something great in my life and now I was a failure. I failed myself, I failed my family, I failed everyone who believed in me and most importantly I failed God. I learned never again to say what I would never do. I was so ashamed. I prayed every day for forgiveness, and it took years before I could forgive myself.

I carried that secret and the guilt of my decision with me like my own cross or scarlet letter to bear. When I received a scholarship to play basketball at a four-year NAIA college, I felt so much shame. I felt I didn't deserve it. All I could remember was what I had sacrificed. When I completed my college career and obtained my degree, there was sadness inside of me. I often wondered if I had been stronger and kept my child, could I have achieved the same outcomes. Looking back, I know now that I still would have been successful just like so many women who found themselves facing the same choice but chose differently. I tormented myself for not being stronger. My shame caused me to work hard so that I could be successful and not allow my decision to be in vain. As doors opened for me, I did not feel that I deserved any of it. People were placed in my life that taught me about forgiveness. As I learned and grew, I began to forgive myself and accept the things that I worked hard for.

By the time I made it to my junior year I was still healing and figuring out who I was. There were times of struggle. It was difficult trying to work while being a student-athlete. I remember times of wanting to give up. Of course, I always had my mother as my cheerleader telling me she believed I could do whatever I set my mind to. It also helped to have people who been where I was. My coach was a great mentor for me. I became friends with a brilliant woman during my junior year. She came from a similar background and had goals to be a successful lawyer. I remember going to her during finals the night before a paper was due. I was panicking because I had not even started to write. I was still in my partying phase and was barely making a 2.0 GPA. If I did not pass the class, which would be determined by this paper, I would be ineligible to play the next semester. She lectured me about how I needed to do better. At the time she was the only peer who cared enough to address my self-destruction. I remember her saying "Frec, (calling me by my nickname) this ain't cute" she told me how she was an Academic All-American when she ran track for the same university that I was attending. I didn't even know what an Academic All-American was. Her speech encouraged me to do better. I respected the advice coming from her because I knew she understood what I was going through. The competitor in me told me that if she could do it, then I could too. Every semester following that I earned a 4.0 GPA and was placed on the Dean's List.

In getting to know and love myself, I sought a deeper understanding of the idea of self-love. Self-love, I have learned, is not allowing myself to be treated any less than the queen that God has made me. Self-love means not to compromise myself for others. It means treating myself as if I am the daughter of the MOST HIGH. It took me some time to embrace this idea.

In my early twenties I received a valuable life lesson about love which taught me a lot about myself. The lesson was that I had to know and love myself first, above all else. The same friend who got on me about my grades continued to be instrumental in other areas of my life. She shared with me a lesson she'd learned from her spiritual father, her pops. She told me that when you are in a relationship, you cannot be a half-person searching for someone to fulfill you, to make you whole. You must be a whole person who connects with another whole person so that the two of you can become one. I had never heard of that before. I had never approached relationships in that way. I engaged in relationships naively. Because I was ignorant and truly without knowledge of who I was. I accepted anything and named it love.

Another intervention came in my final year of college. Everything was catching up to me and I did not feel like I could go on any longer. Finals were killing me! I was lonely, working full-time, and going to school full-time and it was taking a toll. I remember I was considering taking a break from school. I shared my frustrations with my grandma who told my cousin. This is the cousin that is the closest thing that I have to a big sister. We always have honest conversations with each other. So, when she called, I knew she would not hold back on telling me what I needed to hear. I remember during our conversation she told me with all conviction that "quitting is not an option!" I do not think she knows how those five words impacted my life. She encouraged me to keep going when I wanted to give up. To this day, for me, quitting is not an option!

God has called people to speak life into me time and time again. My Godmother is also someone who helps to cover my spirit. She prays for me and with me. She keeps me grounded spiritually during times of struggle. I am blessed to have encouraging people in my life. Everyone needs a support system. I will love these two women forever for how they motivate me.

All these instances caused me to look inside of myself and outward to God to seek direction. These situations were instrumental in me becoming who I am today. I am constantly in a state of learning and changing for the better. As a lifetime student, I will constantly change and grow. I am no longer ashamed of my failures because I have inherited great lessons. I use these lessons to help others.

I remember being told twice in my life, at different times, by complete strangers "God has something great planned for your life." I am not sure that I have reached greatness. The faith that I could be used for a purpose greater than myself keeps me motivated to seek higher levels. In doing so, some things that I used to accept, like, approve of, I no longer do. This can seem strange to those who have been around before I began my journey. I understand how witnessing this change could seem as if I were abandoning or turning my back on where I come from. I assure you this is not the case; my appetite has changed. Honestly, it is not about anyone outside of me. My purpose is not tied to anyone else just as my birth and my death were and will be a journey for me to take on my own.

Everyone with whom I have shared an intimate connection with taught me something. My family has molded me. My environment, my failures, my traumas, my hurts, my losses, my triumphs, my joys, and most importantly my spiritual journey have all collectively influenced who I am today. What I learned about myself through all my challenges in life is that I am resilient; I am self-determined, I am not my mistakes, I have within me the capacity to achieve greatness, I am fearless, I am not perfect, but I strive for perfection, I have a gift to reach others, and I am worthy. I no longer give anyone the ability to control my emotions. I have no time for drama or people who dwell in that space. I still have a fighting spirit but now I fight the good fight. I no longer cover up pain and trauma, I address it so that I can forgive and heal. I share it with others so that I can witness to them and encourage their growth.

Even though I still love to write, I do not have too as much anymore. I have a partner in life who is there to hold things with me when they get too heavy. I have truly solid friends who love and appreciate the person I am. They celebrate me and my accomplishments, and I do the same for them. I have watched God place people in my life that have tools I did not even know I needed until I needed them. I hold those people especially close. I am surrounded by individuals that I can call upon for anything and they will be there especially when I just need someone to listen. I have spiritual parents who pour into me and my family who give me more love than I will ever need. Still, in those moments when I may not want to speak, I write. Not because I don't have anyone to talk to or because I feel alone, but simply because I am inspired to. My prayer is that you too find something that you love and allow God to use it to minister to your soul during your journey in life on your path to becoming the most beautiful version of yourself.

A Little Black Girl Story

Tell me a little black girl story,
A story that does not contain
Welfare, Section 8, and those sorts of things

Tell me a little black girl story,
No finger-snapping, neck rolling, pigtail wearing but
Tell me a little black girl story,
No Double-Dutch or the first word she learned is "bitch,"
so she thinks she tough
Nah,

Tell me a little black girl story,
Not no non-proper English speaking
bubble gum popping, gold teeth having but

Tell me a little black girl story,
Not about 3 plus baby daddy's and
Never been married

We may be able to relate to two or three
But,
This is not our entire story

Don't refer to her as angry
If you knew her story
Might have reason to be

When you tell my story
Be sure to note that
These are not the sum of me
It is just some of me

Tell me a little black girl story,
That also contains,
How she overcame
Some ghetto things, like
Odds that were stacked against her
Deferred dreams and falsified love

Tell me a little black girl story of
Acknowledging but not accepting
And learning from her mistakes
She had the curse of 3 generations to break

Tell me a little black girl story
The first in her family to go to college
And obtain higher knowledge
Seeking nothing but pure things
Educated first ladies,
Multiple degrees
Trips overseas,

Tell me a little black girl story
The glue to the family
Light in her eyes

Success expected, symbols of strength
No weakness or compromise

Tell me a little black girl story
How she gives love and shows grace
With a smile on her face
How she knows that all things are possible
With God
Seeks knowledge and is a symbol of pride

Like:
Harriet Tubman
Madam CJ Walker
Sojourner Truth

Like:
Maya Angelou
Phillis Wheatley and
Oprah Winfrey

Tell me a little black girl story
About how she shall be
As dope as a Delta Pyramid
Or an AKA "Skee-Wee"
As fresh as Madam V.P. Kamala
Walking out to a song by MJB

Tell me how she can slay all day
Tap and ballet
Learn to play
Classical piano or speak foreign languages like.

Comment allez-vous?
Je m'appelle Fareeda, et toi
The sky can't be our limit
When we were born to be a star

See I know my history
But HE showed me
What I have been called to be
Therefore, I cannot submit
To the limits
That you've placed upon me

My standard is perfection
In my quest to be the best
If I fall short
Then I'll be excellent

They laugh at me
And call me naive to believe
That one day soon our daughters
Will too
Have the audacity
To write their own
Magnificent
Little black girl story!

Metamorphosis

I am not who you want me to be
In our time apart you conjectured all kinds of ideas of me
From old memories or your altered realities
But that is not me

I'm not that twelve-year-old with the ponytail and bangs
Nor that twenty-year-old who was naïve to all sorts of things
No that is not me, that is not who I am

It is often those who are closest to you and claim they love
you the most
That restrict you and struggle with your growth
Damn
Let people live
We don't give others the space to grow

That girl was never me,
She was only a fraction of who I was going to be
The "me" I am now you do not know

And before you can get started
My dearly departed, let me warn you...

Do not let it be convenient to blame my evolution on who I
am currently with
They have little to do with it and
I would be surprised if you were so simple-minded

If you think that someone could change me
You never knew me really
To think such a thing would be to paint me as silly
Less than deep-rooted in who I am
That I would let someone else sculpture my presence
To not know how to love someone without allowing them
to change my essence

I understand that my change makes you uncomfortable
And you're trying to find reasons,
I know that it would be easier for me to remain the same
The person that you knew, to remain familiar to you
But butterflies cannot fly if they stay trapped in a cocoon
So,

If you love me, liberate me like Maya said to do
Don't suffocate me and leave me to die
If you love me, you can either mourn the person that you
want me to be
Or mourn our friendship that will be no longer
For a giant to lean on shoulders, her support must be stronger

Love me to my best self
And all that comes within
All lessons, all blessings

Love my humanness
Love me through change
Love me in my growth
Love me despite my mistake
Love me to joy and out of my pain
Love me without restriction
Love every flaw
Love me in Awe

Checklist

What makes me smile;

- ✓ Spirituality
- ✓ Summer days
- ✓ Winter nights
- ✓ Revolutionary poems
- ✓ Love songs
- ✓ Strong women
- ✓ Intelligent men
- ✓ Innocent children
- ✓ Wise elders
- ✓ Gourmet food
- ✓ Memories of loved ones passed on
- ✓ Daydreams of my future
- ✓ Women's college basketball
- ✓ Massages
- ✓ Silent tears
- ✓ Boisterous laughs
- ✓ Late Sunrises
- ✓ Early sunsets
- ✓ Meaningful hugs
- ✓ Long conversations on the phone

- ✓ Rum
- ✓ I find peace in warm breezes and cool rains
- ✓ I love romantic films and hood novels
- ✓ I find joy hearing my son chuckle
- ✓ I enjoy sharing a good laugh with an old friend
- ✓ Thoughts of you

Things I don't like;

- ✓ Ear Infections
- ✓ Paper cuts
- ✓ Body odor
- ✓ Liars
- ✓ Thieves
- ✓ Contentment
- ✓ Females with no class
- ✓ Boys with no chivalry
- ✓ Baby daddies instead of Fathers
- ✓ Disloyal "friends"
- ✓ War
- ✓ Bad hair days
- ✓ Gun violence
- ✓ Winter mornings

Change Agent

It was like a memo that was sent out to all my friends,
Told em I wasn't gonna be able to be reached for a while
Because I had to focus on something with no distractions.

So, when they called, I didn't answer the phone,
Sometimes when they asked to come by,
I would pretend I wasn't home.

See, this was about more than me,
This was about walking across a stage
and accepting a degree,
I had the responsibility of creating history.

Had to be a positive role model for
my younger brothers to see,
Prove to those who said I would never make it here,
That they couldn't control my destiny.

Knowing that just because you're from the
hood doesn't mean you have to stay there,
As we grow older remember dreams that we shared.
Know that in this world life is not always fair,

That's why mama taught us at a young age
to call on God when we're scared.

Over the past year, I had to call on HIM a lot
Knowing at any time God you are all that I got,
But just because I felt weak didn't mean that I could stop.

"Failing Is Not an Option!"

Like I said before, this is not about me,
It's about breaking a curse that's been placed upon a family,
And passed down through generations.

I have to make sure
That the next five generations of
our family will have more,
Something to fight for.

We cannot continue to always settle for less,
Why can't we have the best?
Why shouldn't we want more?

More doctors, and lawyers, and entrepreneur figures
Instead of thugs, drug dealers, and killers.

If that's what my nephew grows up to be
I'll place the blame on me,
If that's all that he ever aspires to be.

I'll be the positive role model,
Hope,
To look outside of their surroundings and overcome.

Get to know your history and know where we come from
Regardless of what your ignorant friends say,
It's not cool to be dumb.

What's cool…is having a savings account
What's cool…is owning property
What's cool…is having an education
And your spirituality

Yes, there is a story behind this smile.
I hope you have a minute because
This may take a while.

You're looking at a woman who grew up in the projects.
Moved to the hood next,
Watched my parents support five kids with
food stamps and welfare checks.

They told me I was "fast" and would have
Three kids, living on Section 8, and I laughed because,
There is a story behind my smile.

Had my life almost taken away twice
By the hands of another,
Lost myself so bad that I tried to find myself in a lover.

Realized I was worthy,
Then learned to love me.
God touched my mind, and I began to see,
Evolved into who, I knew I could be.

Didn't listen to those who said that I couldn't,
Proved wrong everyone who said that I wouldn't,

Discerned the motivation behind those
who told me I shouldn't.

When I stepped into purpose
My whole life changed,
I committed to share with others
How to do the same thing.

Many don't know the story behind my smile,
When you look at me you do not know what you see,
Who the hell knows how a rose grows from concrete?

A perplexed mind set free,
You cannot stop me from being
The change I'm going to be.

Say My Name

My name is Fareeda
It means Unique or Precious Gem
My name is not "Bitch" or "Hoe" or "Trick"

If you'd like to call me anything other than my name
You can call me "Queen"
Just don't forget and let anything less than that
Slip from your lips!

Printed in the United States
by Baker & Taylor Publisher Services